Coloring book for adults and kids amazing cocking image for design

This coloring book is belongs to

____

____

____

KITCHEN
MILK
I can COOKING!
F

how to make
Cupcakes
quick & easy
butter
200g
1 teaspoon
FLOUR
2 1/2 cups
MILK
3 eggs
SUGAR
1/2 cup
1 cup
180°C
15 minutes

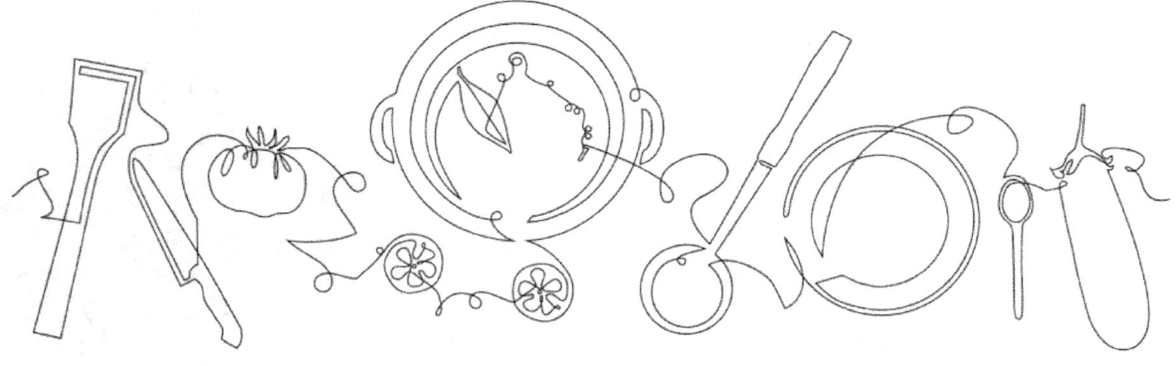

Let's
COOK
together

Restaurant
CLASSIC RECIPES

Love
COOK
ing

Cook
ing

Menu

Cooking
premium

mix taste stir
lemons
1cup
YEAST
oz.
25 min.
glass
tbs.
ts.
FLOUR
1/2 1/3 1/4 2/3
pound baking salted
sugar bake at unsalted butter
ADD Pinch of
salt soda

INGREDIENTS
MIX

JUICE

FLOUR
SUGAR
American cuisine
PANCAKE WITH STRAWBERRY AND BANANA

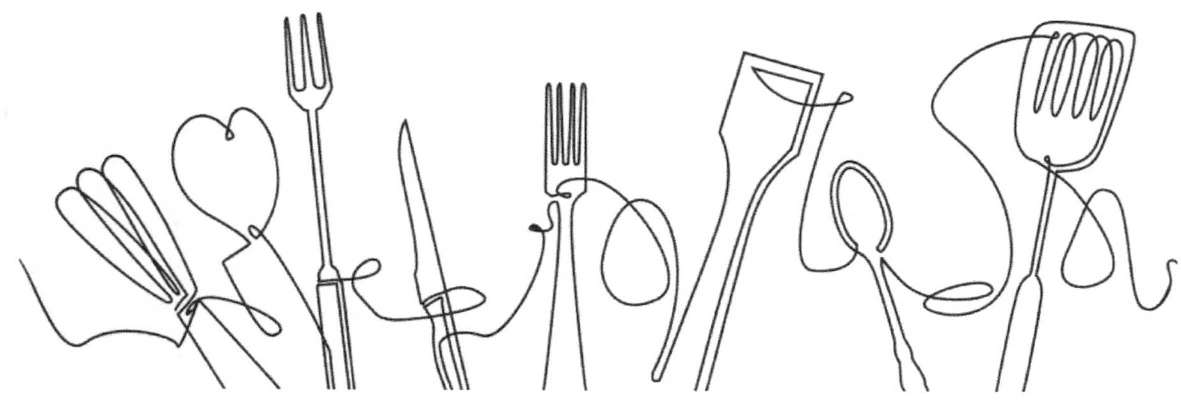

FLOUR
SUGAR
American cuisine
PANCAKE WITH STRAWBERRY AND BANANA

cooking equipment
BAKING STUFF
useful things
SUGAR
VANILLA SUGAR
MILK
BAKING SODA

COOKinG

MILK
I love
BAKING
VANILLA SUGAR
SUGAR
BAKING SODA

HOW TO COOK PORRIDGE

how to make
Cupcakes
quick & easy
butter
200g
1 teaspoon
FLOUR
2 1/2 cups
MILK
3 eggs
SUGAR
1/2 cup
1 cup
180°C
15 minutes

Let's
COOK
together

Restaurant
CLASSIC RECIPES

Love
COOK
ing

COOK
ing

Menu

Cooking
premium

LOVE
Cooking.
Recipe

Chocolate Cake

Kitchen

TEA & DESSERT
CALENDAR SET
sketch and calligraphy

Chocolate Cake

SIMPLE RECIPE

Lemon Pound Cake

SIMPLE RECIPE

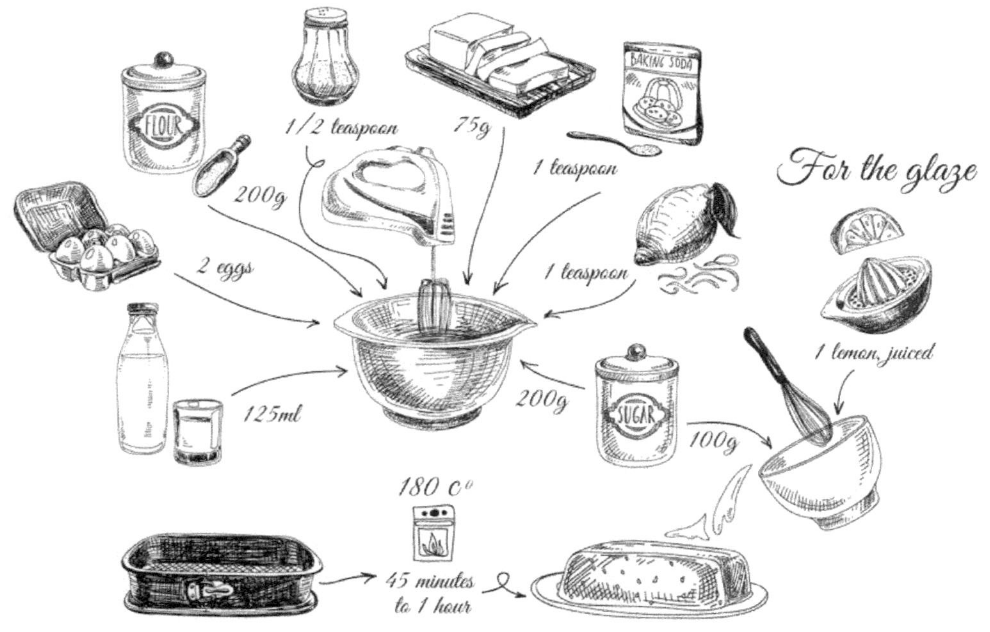

pumpkin soup recipe
thyme
onion garlic
carrot pepper cut
cream water
ginger salt mush
seeds

NOODLE SOUP

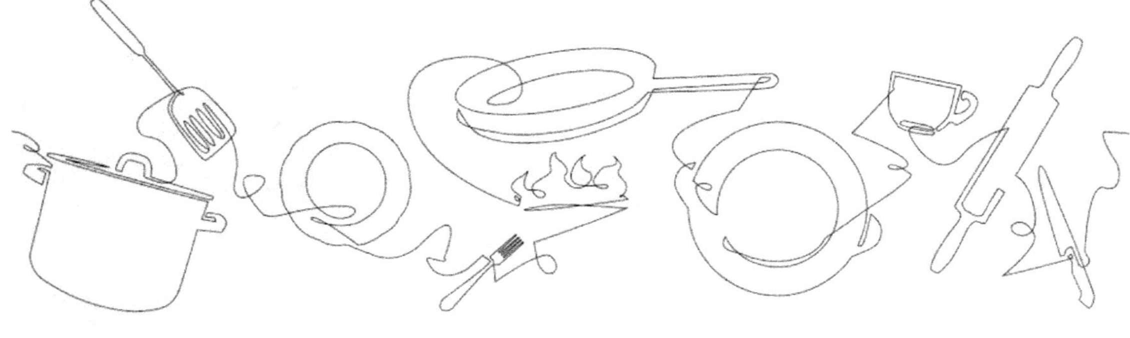

HIGH-TEA

Baked
With
Love

HEALTH
CARE

Fresh
Bread

COOKING
Food
RECIPE
2 l
WHIPPING
CREAM
VINEGAR

~ Doodle Food Set ~